MW00709812

WRITE TO HEAL PROJECT

Debbie Rae Triplett

Foreword and contributions by

Dr. David Mann

Cover design by David Vance

ISBN: 0615806228
ISBN 13: 9780615806228

Printed by CreateSpace, LLC.

Dedication

Moving through the aftermath of my traumatic events was not an easy task. It took courage and a strong support system of friends, family and God to hold me up when I took my first steps – steps that took months, even years.

I was blessed to have an extraordinary group of friends so large that I would need several more pages to name them all. For those who helped in the middle of the night, to those who gave me temporary homes and responded over and over to my need for safety, you are and always will be extraordinary people in my out-of-the-ordinary life.

For all those who have stood strong by my side and supported me, I thank you. Without you, this book would not be possible. I would not be possible.

A special thank you to my sister Dana for her initial edits and feedback on this book.

Finally and most importantly, thank you to my amazing husband. What a testimony of love that you stepped into my life, swept me off my feet and support my past, present and future. You are my life journal. With you, I found my breath and I can finally exhale. Thank you for all your encouragement, belief and inspiration to make The Raye Foundation a place of healing and refuge for me and so many others.

My Sister Speaks of Rivers

A meandering river,
she tells me.
"Don't structure your run in life."

Bend and blend into other bodies,
Stretch into everything but mostly yourself.

Surge in strength.

TABLE OF CONTENTS

FOREWORD

We are all authors and storytellers. Although we may never have a book published, we are writing mental stories about the events of our lives without giving much conscious thought to the process. The events may be joyous, nostalgic, empowering, defeating, painful, or a whole host of other descriptors we might attach to them at the time they occur. The events, whatever type they may be, do not repeat themselves except in the stories we tell ourselves about them. The stories find their way into our everyday living whether we can actually "hear" them or not. People who struggle with depression, anxiety, low self-esteem and body-image problems all are impacted at deep levels by the stories they tell themselves. Unfortunately, most of us are only vaguely aware that these stories are affecting us, and possibly fewer realize they can do much about them.

In *The Write To Heal Project*, the reader is provided with a major resource in accessing and editing their inner story: the journal. Debbie Rae Triplett courageously shares her story of discovery and healing through the use of journaling and offers these revelations to those who would benefit from them. Her helpful tips and techniques, along with personalized examples, provide the reader with practical ways to access their stories. Once the stories of pain, disappointment and disempowerment are exposed to the light of consciousness, readers can embark upon a healing journey.

David P. Mann, Ph.D., LPCC--S
Author of *Open My Heart, Heal My Soul: Living the Grace--Saturated Life*

INTRODUCTION

More than a decade ago, my life unraveled in an abusive marriage. I had to rebuild my life – inside and out. A year or so later (the timing is always foggy), a stranger broke into my apartment in the middle of the night with a weapon and tried to rape me. I had to rebuild my life again – inside and out.

These were two significant events in my life when the woman I was becoming was dying by someone else's hand. So I used my own hand to journal – and I found myself in words. I wrote about the sadness, the anxiety, the fears, frustration, confusion, the anger, the hate. I was able to see my feelings, and that gave me the insight to know what I was battling. I empowered myself through journaling, which inspired me to pick myself up and create healthful habits in re-creating my life.

Whether you've been writing all your life or you see it as a daunting task does not matter. Everyone starts with a blank page. And sometimes it just stares at you.

You stare back at it, wondering exactly what it wants. Its request is simple. It just wants to get to know you. You think about grabbing your pen, but there's no direction or guidelines – just angst about getting started.

Now attach that angst to being a survivor, sitting in a chair with a support group, counseling session or a friend. The survivor is told to journal and dig deep into their soul to spill out all their fears on paper. That is intimidating. And that is usually the perception people have when asked to journal.

I want to help you feel comfortable with writing. I believe everyone can write. I believe everyone can journal, because everyone has thoughts and emotions. It will just take a little guidance, and some tips and fun techniques to get started.

This journal workbook will guide you through the process. Writing is crucial to processing thoughts and emotions. Words create a map in which you can find destinations, pit stops and beautiful sites, but still keep moving in life. Words are your world to travel and discover more about yourself. Our lives are a continuum of changes, shifts and healing. I would like the opportunity to share with you the tools I have picked up along the way.

My life travels have taken me through several traumatic events that left me dangling from a rope, feeling hopeless and exhausted. As a writer, if I could grab on to some words, I knew I could eventually hike myself back up the rope to solid ground. I knew I could land on both feet.

I want you to land on both feet and stay there. Even when you get off balance, you will have a positive landing.

I have been facilitating journaling workshops for nearly 10 years. I have seen the impact on so many lives. I have seen eyes open up, minds become free and hearts soften. One woman wrote me a letter testifying how she became a better mother through the life change that journaling brought. She was able to navigate around her emotional walls and reach through to her children. A man in his early 20s once shared that he had felt lost for years and had no direction after being assaulted. Soon after one workshop, he was able to process and figure out a new life plan and set goals for himself. He went from apathy to achievement.

Just as we are, this book is a work in progress. I fully expect this book to move and grow. You may enjoy all the exercises or only some. It's okay. Just keep writing, find your path and create a steadfast, consistent way to work through whatever it is you are dealing with. Good, bad, ugly or great – it's your life. Feel how you want, write what you want and process what you need. This is your journey. Take a detour, rest for a while, or tour every nook and cranny.

We know words can break us, so let's take this opportunity for words to make us. Your words give you a voice. Your voice gives your strength.

I am inspired by Positive Psychology. In fact, I was focused on positive emotions, traits and institutions a decade before I knew what Positive Psychology was, let alone learned its pillars. What I realized is that "experiences that induced positive emotion cause negative emotion to dissipate rapidly."

Without even realizing it, I was self-inducing an acceptance-based therapy – more importantly (and specifically) a mindful-based cognitive behavioral therapy. Mindfulness is cultivated through awareness and acceptance of your feelings and reactions, but not allowing it to control you. It suggests being "kind and forgiving" to yourself. According to Seligman, scientists have discovered that mindfulness helps to reduce stress levels.

Positive Psychology is a venue where strengths are located and fostered. The overall goal is to empower yourself by believing in yourself. We all have strengths and positive attributes. One way this can be discovered is through artistic measures, specifically journaling.

I am not an expert in the field of Positive Psychology (though someday I hope to be), but I am well-informed and well-versed on Post-Traumatic Stress Disorder, depression and anxiety, and the movement into a healthier mind.

I am an expert in the writing and fitness fields (but still always learning). I am well-informed and well-versed on how to create a healthier physical presence.

With the knowledge of what makes a strong mind and body, I discovered what Authentic Happiness means. I practiced it before I ever knew it was a term. "This idea that people can become happier by bolstering and using

their inherent strengths is central to positive psychology."
According to Seligman, this is a central focus of Positive
Psychology – to help people identity their strengths.

Authentic Happiness takes work. I still have
unhappy moments, but I want to move past those moments
quickly to get back to my happy self. Keep your feet on the
foundations of happiness so you can process and recover
with strong footing.

This journey to healing and happiness begins with
finding your strengths. Words can strengthen. Words can
heal. Simply release the "rules of writing" that you
probably learned. You can misspell, toss grammar aside,
use fragments and crazy punctuation! There are no
boundaries, including lines. Write wherever you want,
however you want: in circles, upside down, diagonally. If
you don't like what you write, tear it out. Rip it up! You
have control over your words. Take it.

When it comes to processing trauma, pushing
through the hurt, pain, fear and anxiety is necessary to
move past it and find Authentic Happiness. Just like any
treatment, there may be some pain involved during the
healing evolution. So let's evolve and move through the
thickness and make it out the other side – the side that is
filled with positive emotions, where we can discover ways
to live happily.

THE BENEFITS OF JOURNALING

Dr. James Pennebaker, psychologist and researcher at the University of Texas at Austin, is the pioneer in the field of journaling. In the mid-1980s, he accidentally discovered the benefits of journaling.

Dr. Pennebaker was conducting research on a group of people who got sick more than others, so he asked everyone to keep a daily record of their activities. After a few months, he discovered those who journaled were not getting sick as much.

After journaling, the researchers observed:
ζ   Less facial tension
ζ   Lower heart rates
ζ   Lower blood pressure
ζ   Strengthened immune cells and general improved health
ζ   Less medical attention needed
ζ   Better interaction with others
ζ   More laughter and engaging conversations

Scientific evidence shows writing uses your full brain. Your left side is analytical and rational. The act of writing accesses the right side of the brain, or the creative part. Writing is creating. Writing opens up all your brainpower and allows for deeper insight, because both sides are working.

Those who journal also can expect a physical impact. A study on nuns who wrote about happy experiences in their lives revealed they lived longer and healthier lives than those who did not express positive emotions.

Another benefit of journaling: It is free! No insurance is needed and it is available anytime you want. It is truly a personal journey of self-healing and the ongoing healing process. This book teaches tools and tips that will help writers avoid getting stuck.

How does it work? It is like learning how to use a power tool. I never thought I would know how to use a drill. I liked the idea, but worried I would drill a hole in my hand. Once my husband took the time to explain and help me learn, I loved how it made projects easier and more enjoyable. I am now the proud owner of my very own power drill – a cute little pink one that my husband often "borrows" because it is more convenient.

This workbook is a process that I have developed over the years through feedback, success stories and flunking moments. Throughout the years, my encounters and interactions have been processed through writing. You will be successful if you want to be. We all have something to say, so simply say it in your journal.

We are all different creatures with different motivations, and this workbook represents the spectrum. I have compiled the most commonly asked questions.

Typing or writing? I believe because writing takes more time, more is able to be processed and produced. But it comes down to what each person is most comfortable with. Tablets, phones and laptops are so accessible today. If they encourage your habit of journaling, then take the electronic route.

Time of day? It is about finding that moment where you know you will remember to write. Keep the journal by the alarm clock, the pot of coffee or the TV remote. Put it in your lunch bag, purse, glove compartment or briefcase. Keep it wherever it feels most safe for you.

How many times in a week? I suggest two to four times a week. Do not worry about how long you journal. Release the pressure of accomplishing this as a task. The goal is to create a habit in baby steps. There is no set formula, as we are all different. It is like any goal: Keep realistic approaches to stay on target.

Drawing? Of course! The front cover of this book shows how I express ideas through oil paintings. If you try painting, drawing, sculpture, photography or another media, then try to write about it. You might find some deeper insight.

THE
FOUNDATION

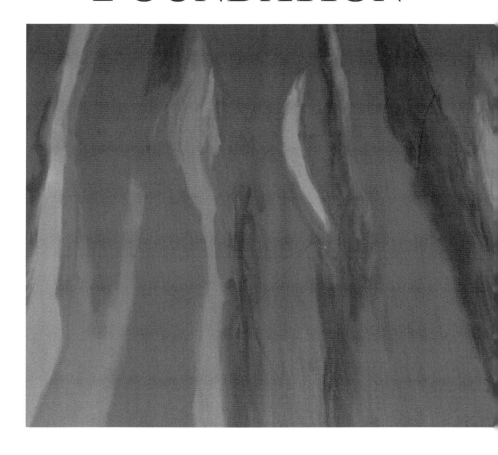

Chapter 1

The Journal Toolkit

"Words are purposes. Words are maps." – Adrienne Rich

WHAT TO EXPECT

The Write to Heal project was constructed through my personal and professional experience of what is successful in workshops geared toward those with Post-Traumatic Stress Syndrome and those recovering from drug and alcohol addiction. Journaling has also proven to be a beneficial process for relationships, work issues and general life stressors. When something affects us, writing is a process that enlightens and empowers.

This workbook is designed to create a pattern for you – a pattern to journal your thoughts and feelings. Throughout the book, the focus is to design a personal avenue of what tools work and what tools do not. We also will focus on sections of self by introducing themes that are part of the healing process.

I considered including blank spaces in this workbook for journaling. Although writing can take place on anything that holds ink, I firmly believe there is freedom in a book that solely holds your thoughts – no one else's, just yours. As you write your words, you are able to see what you are thinking, and that is a powerful process.

While some may purchase a journal, others may choose to make their own and personalize it inside and out. The Raye Foundation will provide a journal to those unable to do either. For more information, e-mail info@RayeFoundation.com.

The workbook is divided into three phases. The first phase is an invitation to have fun with journaling and enjoy the process. The second phase is where the tools learned in the first phase are used to dig a little deeper. The third phase is where the rebuilding happens.

ζ   **The Foundation**. This is where you will learn fundamental techniques to have fun with words and writing. This is where you will learn how to become comfortable with writing. Spend as much time here as needed and revisit it often.

ζ   **Discover Your Story.** This is the working phase where you dig up and build up. This is where a little work takes place. Spend time here to process and accept, but be mindful this segment is a long stretch in the road. We want to move through it to get past it.

ζ   **Retell Your Story.** This is the creation of your hard work Spend a lot of time here. This is where your value and strengths are discovered and have the opportunity to grow. We are what we tell ourselves we are.

Each section includes several chapters. The chapters will introduce processes that will help you regain power in your life, as well as offer new tools and tips to continue the journaling process. Each chapter will highlight a specific exercise, called *A Journal Tool*. Examples of these exercises can be found at the end of each chapter, called *From My Journal*. These examples are included for those who wish to see the technique in action. These examples are part of my process and my story. I have included them as a guide, so feel free to pass them by or use them as needed.

More options on how to use the basic tool for additional journal entries will follow under *Future Pages*.

You will need to be prepared to eventually dig deep in the second phase. There may be exhausting moments, but there will be enlightening, energizing and empowering moments throughout the process. Be ready to look into the past and discover ways to move forward and away from those who have hurt you. If you can be successful in this, you will be successful in fully loving yourself and will uncover paths for your life that you never knew existed. My hope is that you can find the way to Authentic Happiness and live your life to the fullest.

WELCOME TO THE JOURNEY

The blank page. The empty journal. These are spaces begging to be filled. They yearn to be filled with your thoughts, your moments – both strong and weak. These pages crave your pen; they want to hear what you have to say. After all, it is your journal, and your journal is your voice. Your words belong to you. This is a safe haven where no one can silence you. No one can readjust or rephrase or misunderstand or even misguide your words. Your words may be written in any form or fashion.

You speak words. You see words. You read words. You hear words. Now, you need to start writing words. It will be simple and fun with the basic tools that will be introduced in this chapter.

JOURNAL TOOL 1: WORD LIST

Make a list of words. The list can be anything from how you feel to what you see. It can carry a theme or be random. The words can be good, bad, ugly or safe. Use the words to create a sentence and use as many words as you like. You can have as many words as you want, and the entry can be as long as you want.

OBJECTIVE

This exercise makes it easy and accessible to begin your journal entry. The list of words can be created by selecting items around you, by flipping through a book or grocery list, or just by listing a handful of emotions. In the My Tool Chest example, I randomly picked words that felt whimsical. You may have no idea where the words will take you, but go along for the ride.

FUTURE PAGES

ζ   Choose a few lines from your Word List journal entry that you like and want to explore. Use those sentences to begin your next journal entry.

ζ   You can repeat the Word List exercise over and over about an event, a collection of emotions, or a description of self or another person.

FROM MY JOURNAL

WORD LIST
Jeans
Blueberry
Grind
Spice
Laughter
Canister
Grass

I am spice
Smelling of blueberries and laughter
Past scents of grass
Grind into my memory
As I put a lid
On my canister of nightmares
Throw on a pair of jeans
And I'm out the door.

JOURNAL TOOL 2: OBJECT POEM

Choose any object in sight. This can be something around you or even something on you. Describe the object, but do not say what it is.

OBJECTIVE

This exercise offers unlimited avenues to open up a thought process. Any given moment we can look at object and wonder about it. Who made it? How was it created? How long has it been around? This tool allows an exploration of any and every object. Tell its story.

Remember: Have fun! Laughter is a great way to keep introspection on life and to keep the pen moving.

Whenever you feel any emotion and need to map it out, start writing about the objects around you. Fill that blank page with random thoughts about a chair, a lamp, fruit or anything you see.

FUTURE PAGES

ζ   Write about one of your meals. Describe what it looks like and how it makes you feel.

ζ   Write about any vehicle you see: a truck, car, bus, train, motorcycle, cab or bicycle. Describe its function and its appearance.

ζ   Pick any object in any place at any time. Write about what you think its purpose is, then write about other purposes it may have for someone else.

OBJECT POEM

Stained paper of something that is now absorbed as energy.
Some could say it's my addiction, my vice
And criticisms spill out about how I should do this and not that
A part of me steams, perhaps remnants of my morning indulges
I am lightly roasted and take a strong stance to those who speak not of themselves but dice and dissect everyone else.

As I sat in a hotel room in Kansas City working on this book, I noticed the three thick paper cups from my morning coffee. They were exceptionally stained in the creases of this thick paper cylinder. When I chose to use this as my object, I never expected my poem to finish with the perception of other people's judgments. Now this has opened an entire new subject for me to journal about. I know close-minded people are my pet peeve and that can make me angry. Now, I can begin to process the emotions floating around judgmental people and learn how to control the anger that often surfaces. I am making a choice to dig deeper, and that makes me feel stronger and more in control. I did not expect to learn something that day, but the process of writing offered me that unexpected opportunity to grow.

JOURNAL TOOL 3: BORROWED LINES
(from lyrics, books and magazines)

There is always a song. There is always a book. There is always a magazine article, a newspaper ad, a brochure, a menu. For this next exercise, find a line or even a word that is intriguing. Use that line or word to begin a journal entry.

OBJECTIVE

This exercise feeds off the inspiration of others. It is like borrowing a cup of sugar from a neighbor to finish a recipe. Using a line from something of interest is a productive tool that lets someone else pave the road. There is a country song I listen to any time I need to feel stronger. It is a reminder that it is okay not to feel strong, but you must work to get back on your feet. These same lyrics always offer a different perspective, and I usually find a different line to repurpose.

FUTURE PAGES

ζ   When you hear a song that inspires you, find the lyrics. Use those for inspiration.

ζ   If you are reading a book and a sentence hits home with you, highlight it.

ζ   If you hear someone say something remarkable, quote them in your journal and finish the thought.

BORROWED LINES

"Take your best shot" and I'll take mine
I won't go down now, then or any time
You tried to control me but I fought
So I dare you to take another shot

I've got two feet and I will stand
I will be sure to have the upper hand
Now I battle with myself, my mind often torn
But at least I know this strong woman will be reborn.

Is this a masterpiece? No! Will it earn me the title of poet laureate? No – although I can dream. But it did earn me a bit of empowerment. The objective is always writing for *yourself.* You are not writing for others, nor for approval. You are writing to become better.

Journal Tool 4: Random Writing

Start writing about the first thought that comes to mind, or focus on thoughts about the beach, a picnic or any event, past or present. The first few times should be lighthearted, perhaps even silly thoughts. Start writing in your journal and do not take the pen off the paper for three minutes. Even if you write the same word or phrase over and over, keep writing.

Objective

This exercise develops freedom of thought. It is an opportunity to rant and rave about anything and everything without anyone listening (or judging). It can travel a spectrum of emotions and ideas that could take you everywhere or nowhere. The destination is not important. For this exercise, enjoy the journey. Take some detours!

Future Pages

ς   When you discover a topic of interest or recall any event, make a note of it in your journal so you will always have something to write about.

ς   Write about the weather.

ς   Take the last line you've written (or any line you like) and use it to begin your next journal entry.

RANDOM WRITING
Journal, 2012

The snow lies like powdered sugar over the open field. It's where my puppy frolics, sun, rain or sleet or snow. But, it's too cold for me right now. I can't seem to function in the cold. I am frozen. Physically frozen. At least this time it's due to weather conditions and I guess that's better than someone else enforcing the freeze. I am glad I thawed out. Sure, I am warm by the fire, but I am also thawed out in my heart and spirit. I am soft, with a edge of doubt but nothing that would stop me from frolicking in the open field. I still have 30 seconds to write. I should stop once I finished my thought, but I am going to keep writing because you never know what could come up. But, isn't that life? Just when you think you've accomplished enough, you call it quits? I never want to do that. I want to keep pushing past all boundaries.

I will admit as I wrote this in real time while working on this chapter, I was not inspired to randomly write. I was too busy. I was on task. But once I started, I became intrigued by what I was processing. I remembered my days of being frozen, of not being me because I was stuck to the ground. It reminded me of the efforts it took to thaw out and move again. From that, I felt the task was complete. I expected nothing, and if nothing was what I got, then that is fine. But I unexpectedly got something. I pushed beyond that and got even more – and that something more very well could be the start of another journal entry.

Chapter 2

Embrace your emotions

Your lack of planning is not my emergency.

E motions inform. Why do we fear being sad, angry or scared? We often fight the bad feelings because, as humans, we like to focus on the happy stuff. It is okay to feel all those not-so-happy emotions. Give yourself permission to feel them, and refuse to feel guilty for it. Guilt can spur a cyclical battle – you feel bad because you felt bad.

It is far better to embrace the emotion, figure it out through journaling and move on. Sounds simple, but it is not quite that easy. If in the discovery process, an intense emotional response surfaces, consider the possibility to process and move forward toward healing and finding Authentic Happiness.

If your emotions were evoked by a person, write a letter to that person about any ill-willed feelings toward him or her. It is okay to write angry letters, because the words will map out where are you. Be proud that you spoke up – even if you're heard only in the pages of your journal.

If your emotions were evoked by an event, journaling becomes a platform to understand the exact moments despair was felt. This allows a better understanding of triggers. An important suggestion is to be prepared to read what may come out on your pages. At first it may be scary, but you have the power to turn it inside out, reframe it, manage it and witness the empowerment unleash from within.

I will say it again: It is okay to be angry. But what matters is what is done with that anger and how it is managed. It is the process, the recovery and the awareness of what caused the anger that is important. Once the process is complete, graciously move on.

I once was teaching a workshop series, and my class and I were discussing forgiveness. One woman became very irritated. She later shared she was not prepared to talk about forgiveness. She said someday she hopes to unpack all the junk she boxed up, but in that moment, she was not ready. Though she was unable to process forgiveness, her self-awareness kept her focused on the healing evolution and her desire to find happiness.

JOURNAL TOOL 5: Word Rant

Make a list of angry words

Make a list of hateful words

Use the list and rant in your journal for five minutes. Do not stop your pen from moving. If you get stuck on a word, just keep writing that word over and over again until something else flows.

Turn it around.

Make a list of happy words.

Make a list of loving words.

Use this list in the same manner. Now, answer the following questions: Which list felt better to write? Which list would feel better to live with?

OBJECTIVE

This exercise gives you permission to be angry. It allows you to yell with your words, release tension and act out, privately and quietly. This is the place to twist off the top of everything that has been bottled up. Go for it! You have permission!

FUTURE PAGES

ζ   What was the worst gift you have received? Write about why it was so awful.

ζ   **Turn it around.** What was the best gift you ever received?

ζ   What is your biggest pet peeve? Write an angry letter to a person, real or not, and say exactly how you feel about their behavior.

ζ   **Turn it around.** What do you find most endearing when observing others? An old couple holding hands? Two friends laughing over coffee?

FROM MY JOURNAL

WORD RANT

Fight	Normal
No good	Sad
Healing	Resentment
Change	Beaten
Anger	Scars
Hate	Tears

Journal, 2004

I was attacked by a stranger. I thought all people had some amount of good to them; I was wrong. How do I believe? How do I restore faith in humanity? Nothing felt good, looked good, tasted good. There was no good, and the good in me was diminishing in me, too.

My friend told me I needed to sit with my sadness. I need to give myself permission to be sad because perhaps a new me was being created. Another side of her that would make her stronger and better. When was I not going to have to fight and re-create? When could I just sit and stew in me?
That man who broke in attacked my body and mind. I was still healing from the second knee surgery. When was I going to be normal?

What will become of me? I am rediscovering me, but the problem is, this time I have no clue who that me is. I have changed, I am changed and changing from a 10-minute attack.

How can I progress and walk on when I can't even lift my feet? I can't find hope when I am so lost. And I am alone, so I can't even ask for directions. I pull up my Big Girl panties and tell myself to suck it up.
The glass is half empty; in fact, it's being guzzled down at this very moment.

I smile when I think about the days ahead – alone. I will be alone, separated from earthly love because love requires trust. It's not inhuman, it's the cards my life has unfolded. The life I have been told to live because of the scars from ex-husband and my attacker. My heart is torn and beaten up. I am used goods, but at least I am still good to me.

Tears to laughter, laughter turns back to tears. It's the typical response to healing and pain. I've been doing it for over a year. I have nothing more to give; I don't want to give anything more. No more. This girl is finished.

It's time to pack my bags and leave this cow town. Shred this city with my high-heeled boots and walk with my head high, as I pull out my lipstick and write "Outta here" on my forehead to all those who have hurt me.

I don't need any of it. I'll walk with the memories I want. And you may see me walking alone, but look next to me and you still footsteps in the sand.

There comes a time where we must decide we want to acknowledge who is beside you. What is happiness? Getting away from toxic ideals, people and places? The clouds that hang above us are drenched with black. My sky was dripping with dissent. I was standing in my puddle – a puddle that was filled with my past. I was frolicking naked with my scars wide open and my heart to bare to the world that would whip it and scratch it right out of my body. I was going to drown in my puddle. My own past was swallowing me.

On the wait-list of life. Someone decided to cut me off from the outside world and the inside of me. Then I get see all the gross buildup of what's been brewing under my skin.

Living in this skin was no treat. I was struggling to breathe. My breath was lost in translation – in the transfer of what's needed and what was wanted. I was falling deeper and deeper and there was no bottom and no ladder. If there was a hand, I didn't trust it.

Turn it around.

Strong	Sunshine
Heart	Water
Hugs	Love notes
Coffee	Surprises
Kind-hearted	Puppy

Journal, 2012

My heart is strong. It beats strong. It feels strong. It was built on hugs and sunshine. The love notes remind me that I am cared for. Sipping coffee, watching my puppy play is another reminder of simple pleasures and unconditional love. It's no surprise my heart is strong. It swims in water full of kind-hearted friends and family. My heart is strong. I am strong.

Chapter 3

Understanding

"Life is the first gift, love is the second, and understanding the third."
–Marge Piercy

In order to gain a stronger perspective of where you are and where you want to go, understanding on your terms and in your terminology is key. This begins by writing your life story. Expect it to be highly emotional, rough and angry. Expect to filter that through your successes and strengths.

Let your words simmer on the pages until you are ready to read through it. This is an opportunity to sit back and see how you have grown and progressed. Journaling is a powerful tool to "see" your feelings – both good and bad. Once you can see what you are dealing with, it becomes easier to process, and a decision can be made to forgive. It is not always easy, but life can be easier if negative energy is released. Become more and keep becoming.

JOURNAL TOOL 6: WRITE YOUR LIFE STORY

Begin by making a list of life events. These could be moments when you were surprised, changed, uplifted, confused – the list can go on and on. The chronology can come later. Once the list of events is written, describe them. Once described, attach an emotion to each one. Then, when the event and emotions have been described, finish the story. This is your life story. How do you want your story to continue in three months, three years, 10 years and so on?

OBJECTIVE

This exercise is your voice, your story, your life. It is everything about you and who you are. It is where you have been, where you are and where you are going. Revisiting our lives harnesses an understanding of what we have (or have not) accomplished. It is a summary of what you want out of life. If you need additional guidance, go to My Tool Chest under Life Story at the end of this section. I have weaved in questions to help create your story.

FUTURE PAGES

ζ   Write a letter. The first draft is from the heart, where you can say anything you want and express it in any form without revising or filtering your words. The second draft is from the head, where you should refine your words so it becomes productive and constructive for someone else. Share with that person – or not. Save the letter or throw it away.

ζ   Write a letter or a prayer to God.

LIFE STORY
Speech, 2010 (started from a journal entry)
This entry is designed to promote self-reflection through the words and feelings of another. After each segment, there is a question that encourages introspection.

We all have a life story. You are here, and that means you have responded strongly and survived the events in your life. Your journey through this book exemplifies your courage and strength. Each of us also has a fight, flight or freeze response. In my story, my response was to fight off my attacker. But that was not the fight of my life. My toughest fight came in the years that followed -- and still, at times, in the moments I live now.

I had a good life. It was taken from me.
I loved myself. That was taken from me.
I thought I understood humanity. That was stolen from me.
I want. I need to get it back.
And it all happened in one night. A stranger broke into my apartment and attacked me while I was sleeping. I woke to the sound of wind pants running toward my bed. I looked up to see a large man with a hooded sweatshirt lunging on top of me. I began to struggle. He threw me on the floor with a pair of scissors at my neck and threatened to kill me if I didn't stop screaming. He threw me back on the bed and my struggles stop. For a moment, I thought there is no way I can win this. I am pinned down. He has a weapon. He is twice my size.

Then my mind shifted. I told myself I am not a quitter. So instead of struggling, I turned it into a fight. My attacker took off running away and he didn't get what he came for. I won that fight because no matter how hopeless it seemed, I never quit.

I was angry. I was terrified. In a matter of 10 minutes, my life got turned upside down. After the police did their job, I grab my journal and started writing. I wrote an editorial about the attack for the newspaper I worked for. I wrote e-mails to everyone I knew about what happened. And I wrote a letter to "Him."

I thought I had the fight of my life that night. Little did I know my fight would last for the rest of my life, and would be intense and devastating for the next two years.

Take a moment and write down two or three things that felt like the fight of your life.

Several years after my attack, my family asked me to bake their favorite Christmas cookie. As I was in the kitchen measuring out the ingredients, I realized I did not have enough butter to complete the recipe. I panicked. I needed to get to store for more butter, but it was dark outside. I couldn't leave my house. I couldn't make the cookies. So I called my mom and told her that I couldn't bake the cookies because I didn't have enough butter, and it was now night time.

And that was my fight. My struggles were darkness, open windows, pigtails, wind pants. For years I was barricaded by my fears. I was forced to stay within closed walls after dark unless someone was with me. I watched the clock, knowing I had to be home before the sun set. My quality of life had been taken.

Take a moment and write down what you feel has been taken from you.

I didn't like myself very much anymore. I was becoming a stranger to myself, clothed in anger and resentment. I was angry that I couldn't go out with my friends at night. I was angry that I had to sleep with a gun in my hand. I was angry that I looked at every man thinking he was a rapist. I was angry that I couldn't look at hooded sweatshirts or had to run out of a room when I heard the sound of wind pants. I didn't like making the people in my life announce they were coming into a room so I would not be startled. Because if I was taken by surprise, I would throw myself into a ball in the corner of the room and cry.

I hated what he did to me. I hated that he stole me. I hated my life. And like Oprah Winfrey once said, "You cannot hate other people without hating yourself."

Take a moment and write down things you hated or still hate about yourself.
Turn it around. *Write down three things you love about yourself.*

I didn't understand this shift in my life. I didn't understand why it happened to me. Why was I chosen? Why did God send him after me? Should I be angry with God? It was then I realized that I needed to either understand or embrace the fact that I may never know why he picked my apartment and attacked me.

Take a moment and write down what you don't understand about your life.
Turn it around. **Write down a goal you want to accomplish.**

I had a choice to make. I had to get my life back. I had to work hard to rediscover this woman who was beaten down and lost. I created a motto for myself: I don't know when and where I'll land, but I will land on both feet.
Take a moment and write down how it will feel or how it feels landing on both feet.

I was going to love myself again. I still had a job that I loved. I had the support of my family and friends. I had my health. And I just bought a pair of great new boots.

I realized that in order to love myself again, I needed to gain true freedom and forgive my attacker. I realized I had a choice that could make my days become better and brighter by releasing this hate and anger toward him. So I grabbed a crayon and a sheet of construction paper and drew myself under a big sky. It had a big sun and huge, puffy clouds. I decided to choose what sort of things would hang over me. I chose my sky. It was my choice on what would take me out or lift me up. I WAS going to be better and not bitter.

Take a moment and draw a picture of your sky. What does it look like? What are the colors? Are there clouds? Birds? Is the sun out? Feel free to just write about your sky, too.

Author Carl Townsend once said, "All healing is first a healing of the heart."

I discovered along my path that in order to heal, I had to heal my heart. And with so much hurt, anger, resentment and confusion, I was uncertain of how I would get there. Journaling became my map. I was able to discover new paths and uncharted territories through writing out my thoughts and feelings. And this moved my healing journey along. So I wrote another letter to "Him."

Take a few minutes and write exactly what you are feeling right now. What are your thoughts about the lists you wrote earlier?

DISCOVER
YOUR STORY

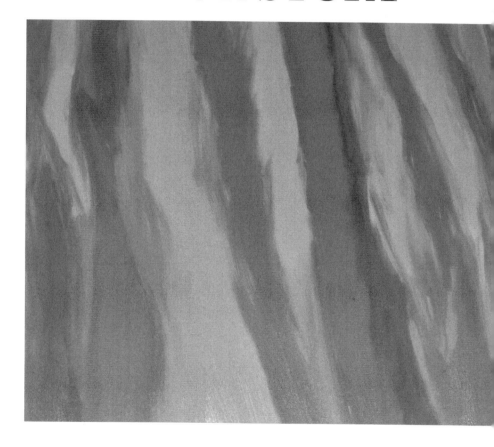

Chapter 4

Forgiveness

Be better, not bitter.

*"You can't hurt the perpetrator by
not forgiving them,
but you can set yourself free by
forgiving."*
- Seligman

T hink back about the story of the woman who became angry with the idea of forgiveness. We have the choice to be better or bitter, but "better" will most likely push the boundaries of trust, safety and openness. Do not expect it to happen overnight, but forgiveness can happen page after page, then journal after journal.

In order to understand what it means to forgive, it is a good idea to explore what it means to love. Some may be able to understand love through God, others through family, and some through friends. As the saying goes: If we cannot love ourselves, then how we can we learn to love others? Even more importantly, how can we understand and embrace anyone's love? I believe that if you can accept and surrender to love, then you can accept the idea of forgiveness. An unwillingness to forgive turns into bitterness. So how does this difficult yet freeing acceptance of forgiveness begin?

Mark McMinn, author of *Psychology, Theology, and Spiritualty,* talks about how "reflection of insight" is part of the forgiving process. There is a necessity to turn inward and process what needs to be forgiven, and that is not always a comfortable feeling. How do we get comfortable? Process. Clean out the junk in the trunk.

Check your inventory. What is *not* affordable to keep? Creating life mottoes is a way to center thoughts and goals and to cope with circumstances. Realize a healthful way of being is important. Realize that love and forgiveness bring freedom. Realize you are lovable and realize forgiveness offers freedom. It takes a lot of energy and time to harbor hard feelings, and eventually it strips away function and power.

JOURNAL TOOL 7: LIFE MOTTOES

Start by thinking of an event that has impacted you or will in the future. Perhaps it is a goal, or it requires change on your part. Next, think of how it makes you feel. Make a list of those words and ideas, then attach emotions beside each one. Formulate short sentences with what you have written. Play around with the phrases and you will find your life motto.

During the ups and downs, flights and falls, there is value in creating life mottoes. This quick exercise immediately offers empowerment and serves as a reminder of where you are and what you need to do. The way to create this motto is to journal out the words trapped inside you. Release them to release yourself.

OBJECTIVE

This exercise is your "go-to" phrase and keeps you grounded. We face life changes and new challenges. Creating a catchphrase is one way to cope with your circumstances. Write it down everywhere – a sticky note on mirrors, wallets, walls or dashboards – until you remember that it is your "silver lining."

FUTURE PAGES

ζ   Create a motto for aspects of life you find challenging. This can be for a short-term goal, long-term goal or a moment in time.

ζ   Help people in your life create a motto. It can be beneficial to observe the inner workings of another.

ζ   Using the "list' method, write down at least 10 words about what makes you feel strong. Use those words and write yourself a letter.

LIFE MOTTOES

I wrote a list of items that are in the forefront of my thoughts: I want to focus more on others. I love positive psychology. It is good to uplift others. I am strong enough (now) to encourage.

My motto: "I will uplift others so I can exercise my strength."

Journal, 2009

Growing up with two older sisters, I thought forgiveness was what I had to do when my big sister took the last cupcake. My parents encouraged forgiveness, but it seemed society suggested that I take the last cupcake next time, or find ways to get back at my sister. But given that she was my big sister and I did love her, and she scared the crap out of me, I chose to forgive her.

And 20-some years later, she is my best friend and would rip the head off of anyone who tried to take the last cupcake from me.

Robert Muller, former assistant secretary-general of the United Nations, wrote, "To forgive is the highest, most beautiful form of love. In return, you will receive untold peace and happiness."

Learning how to forgive is not easy. Perhaps you had parents or grandparents who encouraged it, or a teacher or your minister. Or perhaps you were surrounded with ideas of seeking revenge when someone does you wrong. Think about how many times have we heard, "Don't get mad, get even." I never wanted to hold grudges because I knew they would fester inside me and would grow into a massive ball of ugliness.

But the one thing I have learned in my journey is to be better and not bitter.

Chapter 5

Rebuilding

I don't know when or where I am going to land, but I know I will land on both feet.

When foundations get shaken and torn down, it is hard to find a safe place to stand, a safe place to live, no place to be and no place in sight. Feet can start sinking or step forward and get moving. It might not be certain when or where you will land, but you will land on both feet.

Create a vision for yourself and search for that landing spot. This requires a map – a map of yourself. In this journey, we will not be packing our baggage, but unpacking.

Unfold fears and be prepared to launder them. Find triggers and line them up to see them clearly. Most of all, rediscover favorite memories and wrap yourself up in them to feel comforted and safe.

JOURNAL TOOL 8: WEEDING

It is important to understand why certain things trigger a fearful response, or one that could debilitate you. If you are not prepared to walk this road, give yourself permission to skip this tool and return when you are ready. If you are, have someone prepared to talk to you, whether a counselor or a friend.

Everyone needs a place to land on both feet. Finding the right spot will take some hard work, but keep looking and fighting for it. The more you write, the more you will discover.

OBJECTIVE

This exercise asks you to look deeper and weed out some junk. Are there roots so entangled that they are preventing health and nourishment to your well-being? This exercise will identify some areas that could use some detangling and uprooting. Once you pull them up, you can bag them and toss them out. Shed yourself of things that weigh you down. You deserve a lighter load.

FUTURE PAGES

ζ   Begin to write about smaller fears, such as spiders or thunderstorms.

ζ   Make a list of the bigger fears. Decide if you want to dig deeper and begin writing.

WEEDING

Journal, 2006

For the first few weeks, I couldn't stay in any house alone. I couldn't walk into a room alone. I couldn't stand the darkness. Tears and screams would wake me in the night. For nearly two months I couldn't sleep alone. Three months later, I stayed a night or two alone a week. My proctor: A borrowed gun.

I would sleep at the front door with that gun, waking the minute my eyelids shut. I would walk around my new apartment, looking in the closets, up the chimney, making sure my attacker wasn't coming in, or climbing up my balcony.

I was on the second floor. He couldn't get in through the windows this time, unless he had a ladder. He would have to bust through my front door, through a dead bolt, two hotel locks and a door jammer. If he got through that, then he would have to get through my locked bedroom door that also had a door jammer on it.

Was I safe?

No. I didn't feel it at all. I would hysterically cry in my bed at night. With my cell phone, my land line, the gun, scissors, bear spray and a stick.

Was I safe?

No. And there was nothing I could do about it. Time's potion was the only thing that was going to make me feel safe. And I had no clue when I would drink of that potion, for I was just drinking poison from the past.

Chapter 6

Discovering

*You don't have to feel strong
to be strong.*

E veryone has days when they feel they don't have the strength to do anything, but they know they have to. A mother who is sick and feels weak still takes care of her children. A business person may be nervous about giving a presentation for an important meeting, even though he or she has prepared and rehearsed. The best foot, the strong foot, is put forward because the outcome is much better than grass growing under feet. Acting the part when not feeling the part is a path to strength.

JOURNAL TOOL 9: MY FUTURE SELF
This entry begins by identifying your dreams and goals. Pick a place where you want to be and write as if you are already there.

OBJECTIVE
This exercise is asking you to dream. It is asking you to reach for the things you want and write out the directions on how to get there. See your destiny. In the middle of storms or even stagnant waters, your strength can be built on future hopes.

FUTURE PAGES

ζ   Write an article about what you have accomplished in the future.

MY FUTURE SELF
Journal, 2002

My dust is still settling. Fragments
Of my life still float around just waiting
Until the right moment to settle
This doesn't mean I am unsettled, just parts of me aren't
complete.
We complete tasks, projects, homework, e-mails. But
Do we ever complete ourselves?
If you think you can, you are underbaked and
Have lost your mind.
I will pick small battles and not go to war and end up
maimed, wounded or
Worse yet ... missing in action, which is worse than death.
Fight for the good.
Pardon the mess of those who fight everything, including
themselves.
Their world is one big dusty place and I am
Allergic to dusty people. They make me itch.
The only perfect way to live is to shake off the dust.

Chapter 7

Acceptance

Please excuse my mess, I'm under construction.

I am water. I move. I ebb and flow. I meander. I am clear and I am clean. But stir me up and see what comes up.

We are not perfect, but we are growing perfectly. Celebrating successes or milestones is a wonderful way to celebrate ourselves. Who is our self? It is the person sitting inside us who does not need to run errands or submit a business plan. It is the person who just sits and waits for us once we settle from being overwhelmingly busy. How often does that come along? Give permission to have quiet time. Be willing to see and accept what gets stirred up.

JOURNAL TOOL 10: REINVENTION

Draw three circles in your journal that intersect, like this:

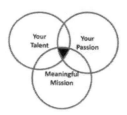

In each circle, make a list of your interests that correlates with each theme.

Questions to ask:
Talents: What am I good at?
Passions: What do I love to do?
Mission: How can I do these things regularly and what would it take to get there?

Journal what you are feeling and thinking after you have completed your circles.

OBJECTIVE

This exercise helps identify your strengths and passions. Often we spend so much time digging and excavating that we need to take a breath and value our amazing talents. Once you find your center circle, start brainstorming some ideas that will get you there.

FUTURE PAGES

ζ   Check in with yourself and revisit your circles every couple of months. Write about your progression, regression or standstill.

ζ   Write about what it would feel like to live in the intersection of the three circles.

REINVENTION

I celebrate that I did not quit life, but that I put an end to the mental anguish. I knew my mission had become to "fight for the good" and to keep growing and stay passionate unto myself. My talent is my words. My mission is to overcome anything and everything for the rest of my life. My passion is to help others.

Journal, 2001

I write to relieve myself of my past
Present and to solidify my future
Or at least acknowledge where I'm headed
I waver in my own beliefs of good and evil
I stand
One-legged on my fence of morals
Sharp edges digging in my heels as a reminder to decide
When I jump, I want to be caught
Open arms waiting
But, that doesn't suggest independence.
I shall have a solitary jump
What catches me should be my belief in doing what is right
Stand over and on pressure
Press down and stomp out those doubts that haunt,
That taunt me.
My confidence builds to crumble
To build again
Reinforcements to strengthen pillars,
That friendly check-in, the offering of a mother's prayer, a
sweet kiss.

Journal, 2003

I am still breathing, then it must not have killed me. It meaning life.
Referring to the death of the mind, of the Mental, of the self – things that embody me, but not my body.

Journal, 2009

Who am I and where I am going is unstoppable.
Try to tear me up and I'll stitch myself back together.
Try to trip me up and I'll bounce back even higher.
Try to tether me and I'll stretch myself even further.

My passion is me. Me for others.
My talents are for the betterment of others.
My mission is for me and for others, for the betterment of all.

TELL YOUR STORY

Chapter 8

Finding your voice

If you are dealing with your junk, don't bury me in it.

Life can be junkyard, but that does not mean anyone should live in one, let alone invite others to it.

I once heard Maya Angelou speak at a conference in Washington, D.C. Physically frail, celebrating her 83rd birthday that day, her mind was strong and powerful. Her words exalted through mighty breaths and effort, but she was heard. She had a confident voice.

She shared a story about how she was raped as a little girl. After the man served an inconsequential jail sentence, he was murdered on his way home. Angelou said she believed he was killed because she used her voice to speak against him. And so she silenced herself for six years.

Imagine if Angelou allowed someone to steal her voice and her words forever? Her impact – for womankind, for empowerment, for culture, for life – would be absent from this world.

Become present and become the person you were destined to be. Find your voice in writing; rediscover the beautiful things about you, inside and out. Begin the journey.

JOURNAL TOOL 11: SAVORING

Think of a favorite memory. Maybe you were laughing. Maybe it was an athletic event in which you excelled, or an assignment on which you got high marks. Write the story.

Now make a word list of the feelings that surfaced while you were writing the story. Using those words, write about yourself and what you have to have offer to yourself and others.

OBJECTIVE

This exercise is your pillar that will hold you up in moments of weakness or sadness. It is a reminder that you are wonderful and have much to offer. Bookmark this entry in your journal, or make a copy of it so you can easily access the amazing things about yourself. A good giggle and fuzzy feeling can be an uplifting moment.

FUTURE PAGES

ζ   When you have a fun moment with yourself or anyone, write the story. It also can be a place to revisit when a pick-me-up is needed. Have fun writing it …
maybe even embellish!

ζ   Write your life as a musical. Make it super silly. You are the only one reading it, remember? Maybe add a dance!

FROM MY JOURNAL

SAVORING

I was behind on laundry. In the moment of wanting to quit, I decided to make my life into a musical performance. As I spun through the house singing about dirty laundry, my dance moves with flinging towels and full baskets were props to my debut.

I was behind on life. In the moment of wanting to quit, I decided to make my life into a musical performance. As I spun through the house singing about the woes of my world, I danced. I flung the stress and emptied my load. Props to my debut.

Chapter 9

Empowerment

Step forward or step aside.
If it's going to get me, it'll get me. I can't stop it, but I can fight it.

E veryone has a list of weaknesses and strengths. The objective is to accept them and focus on the strengths. There will be endless opportunities for growth and empowerment.

For example, I am directionally challenged. I have no clue which way is north. Once, I was told to make one right turn. I did not write it down and made a left turn. It was not until three hours later, when I crossed a bridge into another state, that I realized I had made a wrong turn. I accept that even a GPS will not save me at times. But knowing my weakness, I can put all the pillars in place for a safe journey (such as my husband, who, with my urging, put a tracking device on my phone).

I have to take precautions and necessary steps to empower myself when it comes to driving, but I first had to realize and admit my inability to understand directions. I had to accept what I could *not* do so I could do what I knew I could do. I focused on being resourceful.

It seems to be easy to overanalyze a bad situation and underanalyze a good one. Empowerment comes from overanalyzing the good situation and celebrating the strengths.

JOURNAL TOOL 12: POWER MOMENT

Recall one of your earliest moments that you felt strong and sure. It could be from childhood, when you first learned how to ride a bike, build a go-cart or bake your first batch of brownies. Or perhaps your memory comes from later in life – your first job, apartment or vacation that you worked so hard to achieve. Revisit that moment in your journal and share how it felt to accomplish something. Write the story.

OBJECTIVE

This exercise focuses on our fundamental strengths. It demonstrates our resourcefulness when we wanted it and needed it. These moments will continue to come throughout your life. Capture them.

FUTURE PAGES

ζ   Recall other "Power Moments" in your life. Maybe it was getting a job or a promotion. Perhaps it was running your first 5K. Write about a moment in your adult life that empowered you.

ζ   Think of a recent milestone "Power Moment." No matter how small, find a time in the last month when you felt like you made a difference. It could be holding the door open for someone who needed it, helping a friend move, or taking one for the team.

POWER MOMENT

Journal, 2005

My life wrapped in Ace bandages and police reports wasn't going to rub me raw, but polish me.

If I shed the notion of what it should be, then I can see what it could be. Believing in more than what is seen is a faith that surpasses my understanding and times like this – surpasses my reach. If I could see through walls; if I could float; if I could be invisible – I could be untouchable to even Fate itself. Nothing could get me, hurt me.

But after the attack, I learned that if it's going to get me, it's going to get me. I can't stop it, only fight it. And that's what I'd do for the rest of my life, no matter what. Fight it. Whatever "it" that may be, I won't stop until I win or it runs. I believe in belief. I know I can create more for myself my simply having faith in myself. Faith in God.

Months of struggle with trying to feel normal again – feeling again. Not being scared, or tormented.

Chapter 10

Loving

Share the love, not the funk.

If I want to love another, I must first love myself.

I will not be any good to anybody until I am good to myself.

Love is one of the most powerful emotions. It drives all action, toward others and ourselves. We love certain foods, certain entertainment, certain clothes, certain activities and hobbies – the list could go on and on.

As simple as love is, it is also complex. If it were so easy, it would not be so hard to love ourselves at times. This euphoria is ours to capture if we pursue it.

This is an opportunity to celebrate yourself. Find your strengths and learn about what makes you loved.

Love is experienced in many ways. It can come from pets, family, children, friends, pastors and God. Focus on those experiences.

JOURNAL TOOL 13: LOVE BUBBLES
Make a checklist of the following:

✓   Positive words that would describe you – and include what others would say about you.

✓   Three of your strengths and best qualities – what would a close friend say?

✓   What lifts you up and what makes your day brighter … a person, a place, a special food, an event?

Now use that list and formulate some sentences and begin to write a love letter to yourself.

OBJECTIVE

This exercise focuses on what I feel is the most important thing in this world: love. I believe love can help us overcome nearly all things. This love can be from God, others, or the love we have for ourselves. Love must be accepted for it to do its work. Love works to heal and to help so we can hand it off, hand it down and walk hand in hand. In this journal entry, learn about love.

FUTURE PAGES

ζ   Write or draw your perfect day.

ζ   Think of your happiest memory, when you felt the strongest.

ζ   Write a letter to someone who represents love to you: family member, friend, spouse, God.

LOVE BUBBLES

Positive words
Compassionate
Strong
Feisty
Dedicated
Best qualities
Loving

Creative
Caring
Encouragin
g

What lifts me up
Love
Water

Journal, 2010

I am a dedicated woman
Strong in my love for myself, my husband
I never thought I could be strong enough to love another
- to marry another.
I have coached myself through pain and creatively move
through healing
Strong is not just being independent but accepting
dependence:
A shoulder, a heart, a hand
Move through water
Move through writing
Move into me

Chapter 11

Evolution

Choose your sky.

Wherever you are in life, processing each step through writing ultimately will lead to both feet landing. It will take hard work. It will take a commitment to get better, but as one foot moves forward, the other will follow. If there is a standstill moment, embrace the rest. Step by step and mile by mile, enjoy the journey of self-exploration where the most amazing destination awaits – a place of safety, security, assurance, healing and, most importantly, Authentic Happiness.

Hardships and struggles will be part of life. Laughter and uplifting moments will certainly be part of life. Focus on the roads traveled and the successes along the way.

JOURNAL TOOL 14: CATCH PHRASE

Writing forces introspection. Buff and shine yourself. Name one thing you love, and use that to begin a list of phrases. For example, I love my journals. I begin, "My journal is…" You can take one of those phrases and begin a whole new page.

OBJECTIVE

This exercise is a simple way to look inward with love. Understanding why something is loved creates knowledge of what love looks and feels like. Evolve through appreciation and recognition of the little stuff in order to get to the big stuff.

FUTURE PAGES

ζ   Phrase: Eating ice cream…

ζ   Phrase: Water feels…

ζ   Phrase: My shoes are…

CATCH PHRASE

My journal is:

My glass of wine
My comfort meal
My ice cream cone with rainbow sprinkles
My glass case
My map
My windmill

My journal is my glass case. I can peer in and see where I've been and what I've done. When I feel guilty that I haven't done enough, I look into my glass case and see the trophies, ribbons and certificates of achievement that are written in each page. I see smudge marks on the glass but I see past them for what lies inside.

You can do this technique with something silly, something that empowers you, or something you want to change.

For example: Being late
Being late is like a fly crawling on my skin.
Being late is like sitting in the front pew and cracking your gum.
Being late is when forgiveness is expected by the upper hand – and you do.

Chapter 12

Words, words and more words

My voice will never be silenced. For when I am quiet, I am merely resting.

S elf-care is nourishment to your spirit. It refreshes your mind, your strength and your body. See the power of the words written by Adrienne Rich: "Words are purposes. Words are maps." Words are everywhere – whether they are seen or whether they are hidden. Keep your voice strong through the practice of journaling.

You are just beginning. Whether you did all the exercises, some or none, if you came out on this page, then you have worked through a lot of stuff. More importantly, you were looking for something more. Perhaps it was the search for Authentic Happiness, and hopefully you are on your way.

You should be proud of how strong and courageous you are. As you move forward in introspective work, I encourage you to revisit this workbook and reapply the exercises to any area of your life. Pass it along to that business person or student, or anyone who needs a bit of guidance in their life.

The ultimate goal is to encourage the philosophy of Positive Psychology, so every day can be full of happiness, love and self-worth. Empowerment is life-sustaining.

JOURNAL TOOL 15: ANCHORING

OBJECTIVE

This exercise is evidence of the insight and skills cultivated by working through this book. Tools have been introduced and you have been taught to use them. Grab a pen and open up that journal. It is a blank page. You know the strength of your voice, and your words soon will fill in those pages.

FUTURE PAGES

ζ   Write to feel.

ζ   Write to heal.

ζ   Write because you can.

FROM MY JOURNAL

ANCHORING

I will speak for me and always me
I will speak up always
I am always me
My voice falters and it falls flat
But I'll strain to speak
If I must be a voice for
Me, for you, for anyone
Who has yet to find those
Words, words and more words

ABOUT THE AUTHOR

As I mostly facilitate to survivors, co-survivors and providers of those dealing with sexual and domestic violence, I hear many success stories from friends and co-workers who journal just because. According to them, their lives have more clarity because the pen looks inward. Their self-reflection, self-awareness and self-esteem grow.

I've been writing since I can remember. As a 7-year-old girl, I started writing in my diary about my secret boy crushes, how my sister stole my bubble gum and how I roasted marshmallows with my grandfather over a campfire.

I have notebooks full of teenage poetry where rhyming *love*, *dove* and *above* filled nearly every page. I have bins full of college papers, newspaper clippings and love letters alongside Dear John letters. I have scraps of poetry scribbled on napkins, gum wrappers, church bulletins and torn-out pages that I believed held the secret to unlocking my soul.

I captured silly moments, mad moments and precious moments with words. It all became a collection of words that I formulated into something tangible. As I grew up, I matured into writing poetry, short stories and essays. But I always returned to my journal and netted every and any moment I could, because that was part of who I was and what may influence me.

I always found my voice again through journaling and rediscovered it. When my past tried to silence me, no one could silence my pen. I wrote and wrote – sometimes about nothing. I have journal entries about nose hairs, apple stickers and tampons – and that's just a small smattering.

As I went through traumatic times, it was not easy to write down and see the frightening disaster that overwhelmed and consumed my thoughts. It was not easy to be reminded of the fearfully devastating moments I had to endure. But I knew to get through it, I had to go through it.

Finding my place to land was an ongoing battle. I was scared to sit for too long because something was going to get me. I fought that fear. I had to face that fear. And the only way I could identify that fear is writing incessantly. I desperately wanted to move past that.

I had a choice to make: Do I want to be better or bitter? If I chose to be bitter about my ex-husband or my attacker, I am not sure I would have the opportunities I have in life. And I am sure I would not have been able to teach writing workshops and meet thousands of women who were inspired to overcome, which continually inspires me.

I know God has guided me through this life and my traumas. I have leaned on his understanding and patience. So many times I thought I was undeserving of his unconditional love and forgiveness. But it was through knowing him and accepting those things that I took the ultimate journey of a lifetime.

ARTWORK

The artwork throughout the book is oil paintings by Debbie. She taught herself how to oil paint as another method of self-care and self-healing. Her art speaks to current life situations and is her refuge. The three-canvas series pictured in this book is titled "In Flight." They were painted for her husband Larry Triplett's nonprofit organization The Muskingum County Business Incubator, a 501(c)3. He dedicates his life to helping people make their dreams come to life through mentoring, education and encouragement to entrepreneurs. Wherever we are in the process of life, as long as we stay in flight, we will eventually get to our destination. Here's to always landing on both feet!

BIBLIOGRAPHY

Ince, Susan, and Ronald D. Siegel. *Positive Psychology: Harnessing the Power of Happiness, Mindfulness, and Personal Strength*. Boston, MA.: Harvard Medical School, 2011. Print.

Pennebaker, James, PhD, (2005) *Feature Story: Writing to Heal: Research Shows Writing about Emotional Experiences Can Have Tangible Health Benefits*. Rretrieved from source: http://www.utexas.edu/features/2005/writing/

Piercy, Marge. (1988). "Gone to Soldiers."

Purcell, Maud. (2006). "The Health Benefits of Journaling." Psych Central. *Retrieved on April 11, 2013, from http://psychcentral.com/lib/2006/the-health-benefits-of-journaling/*

McMinn, M. (2011). *Psychology, theology, and spirituality in Christian counseling*. (revised ed.). Tyndale.

Muller, Robert. (1989) Excerpts from acceptance speech by Muller, as the Laureate of the UNESCO Prize for Peace Education, "To Forgive."

Seligman, Martin E. P. *Authentic Happiness: Using the New Positive Psychology to Realize Your Potential for Lasting Fulfillment*. New York: Free, 2004. Print.

Sugarland. (2004). *Twice the Speed of Life*, "Stand Back Up."

5984655R00056

Made in the USA
San Bernardino, CA
27 November 2013